This Book Belongs To

hello Layla hey

a b

a b c d e

Layla has cute Lovely brown hair wich

Printed in Great Britain
by Amazon

53349812R00066